How Do Organisms Reproduce and Adapt?

Houghton Mifflin Harcourt™

PHOTOGRAPHY CREDITS: COVER ©Steve Winter/National Geographic/Getty Images; 3 (b) ©Ryan McVay/Stone/Getty Images; 5 (tr) ©Authenticated News/Getty Images; 7 (tl) ©Emilio Ereza/age fotostock; 7 (br) ©V. J. Matthew/Shutterstock; 7 (tr) ©Emilio Ereza/age fotostock; 7 (bl) ©Emilio Ereza/age fotostock; 8 (b) ©rSnapshotPhotos/Shutterstock; 9 (tl) William Leaman / Alamy; 9 (tr) ©ZUMA Press, Inc./Alamy; 10 (b) ©Steve Winter/National Geographic/Getty Images; 11 (br) ©Kirsanov Valeriy Vladimirovich/Shutterstock; 11 (tr) ©Joseph Van Os/Getty Images; 11 (cr) Don Farrall/Photodisc/Getty Images; 12 (b) ©Gerry Ellis/Digital Vision/Getty Images; 13 (tl) ©Eric Isselee/Shutterstock; 14 (b) ©Paul Nicklen/National Geographic/Getty Images; 15 (t) ©Jake Cunliffe/Shutterstock; 16 (tl) ©DJTaylor/Shutterstock; 16 (tc) ©Eric Isselee/Shutterstock; 16 (t) ©Eric Isselee/Shutterstock; 16 (tr) ©Geoff Dann/Dorling Kindersley/Getty Images; 16 (b) ©Hintau Aliaksei/Shutterstock; 17 (t) ©Martin Good/Shutterstock; 19 (tr) ©Barbara Müller-Walter (Jorbasa)/Getty Images; 19 (tl) © Eric Gevaert / Alamy; 19 (tc) Robert Marien/Corbis; 20 (t) ©A & J Visage/Alamy Images; 20 (bl) ©Nigel Cattlin/Alamy Images; 20 (br) ©NaturePics/Alamy Images; 21 (bl) ©Corbis; 21 (t) ©Digital Vision/Getty Images; 21 (br) ©Dr. Morley Read/Shutterstock

Printed in China

ISBN: 978-0-544-07357-9

21 22 23 0940 21 20 19 18

4500744966   B C D E F G

Be an Active Reader!

Look at these words.

gene	adaptation
inherited traits	instinct
dominant trait	life cycle
recessive trait	complete metamorphosis
innate behaviors	incomplete metamorphosis
learned behaviors	

Look for answers to these questions.

Where do your traits come from?

How do living things pass traits to their offspring?

What did Gregor Mendel find out?

What are dominant and recessive traits?

What are innate and learned behaviors?

What factors determine the adaptations of living things?

How are form and function related?

What are behavioral adaptations?

How do animals grow and develop?

What is complete metamorphosis?

What is incomplete metamorphosis?

Where do your traits come from?

In one important way, you're like the answer to an addition problem. You're the sum of all your traits, or characteristics. No one else in all the world has the exact same collection of traits. Many people have the same hair color as you, but hair color is just one trait. People may have the same eye color as you, but that's just one trait, too. Even if you have an identical twin, you and your twin are two different people. People who know you well can tell you apart.

Your traits come from two places. You inherit some traits from your parents. You take on other traits during your life.

These people have many different traits that you can see. They have even more traits that you can't see.

How do living things pass traits to their offspring?

Most of your physical traits, such as hair color and height, came from your parents. Organisms pass their traits on through genes. A gene contains information that controls or influences the makeup of a living thing. Genes are found within cells. Genes contain the basic information that makes you the person you are.

Traits passed down through genes are called inherited traits. In humans, most inherited traits are physical traits, such as freckles or curly hair. Humans also inherit some behavioral traits, however, such as handedness. What that means is that you inherit your tendency to use one hand more than the other.

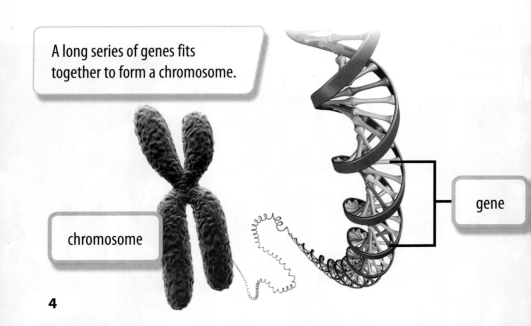

A long series of genes fits together to form a chromosome.

chromosome

gene

What did Gregor Mendel find out?

For thousands of years, people have known that parents pass traits on to their offspring. Farmers learned how to use this knowledge. For example, a farmer who wanted to breed woollier sheep would use the woolliest rams and ewes.

Scientists did not understand how traits were inherited until the late 1800s. A monk named Gregor Mendel bred pea plants in experiments between 1856 and 1863. He

Gregor Mendel is known as the father of genetics because of his work with pea plants.

kept track of the traits of the parent plants and their offspring. For example, he tracked the color of the pea pods—green or yellow. He found he could predict the number of offspring with green pods and the number with yellow pods. His predictions were very close to the actual numbers.

What are dominant and recessive traits?

Mendel had some pea plants that only produced tall offspring and some that only produced short offspring. He used one tall plant and one short plant as parents. You might expect that half of the offspring would be tall plants and the other half would be short plants. But that was not the case. Mendel got only tall plants. He concluded that when there are two options for a trait, one option usually wins. It's as if that one option has the deciding vote.

The trait that is observed in offspring is called the dominant trait. The other trait is called the recessive trait. Mendel learned that recessive traits don't go away. When two tall offspring of a short parent and a tall parent produced new plants, about ¼ of the new plants were short.

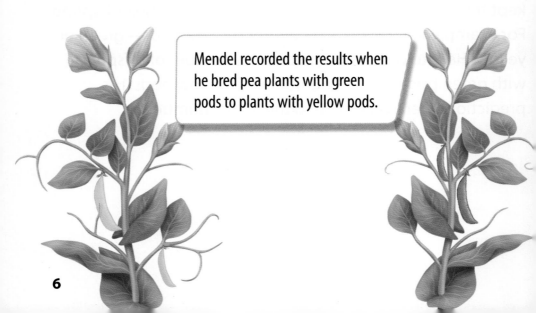

Mendel recorded the results when he bred pea plants with green pods to plants with yellow pods.

Mendel also concluded that each trait was controlled by two factors. You can see how the factors work in African violets. In these plants, purple flowers are a dominant trait. White flowers are recessive. A plant with white flowers has two white factors. A plant with purple flowers can have two purple factors. Or it can have a purple factor and a white factor.

We can use a tool called a Punnett square to show the chances that offspring will have a dominant or a recessive trait. In a Punnett square, the factors of the parent plants appear across the top of the square and along the left side. In the Punnett square example below, each parent plant is purple. It has one purple factor (P) and one white factor (p).

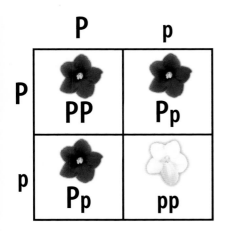

Out of four offspring, three will have purple flowers. Two of those will carry the factor for white flowers.

What are innate and learned behaviors?

In addition to physical traits, you have behavioral traits, or ways of acting. For instance, you know how to count, and you blink your eyes. Some behavioral traits are innate behaviors. You inherited them from your parents without having to learn them. Crying is an innate behavior. When you were born, you already knew how to cry. No one had to teach you.

Other behaviors are learned behaviors. You weren't born knowing how to do them. You had to learn how. When you were born, you didn't know how to talk. You had to learn by listening to the people around you and by practicing. Talking is a learned behavior.

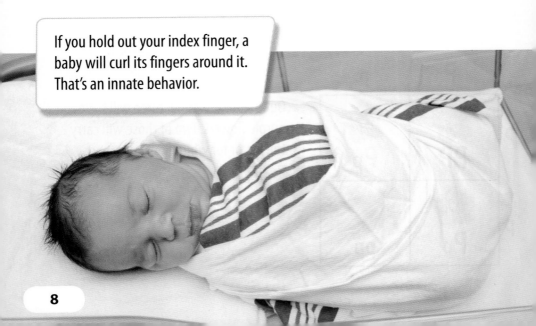

If you hold out your index finger, a baby will curl its fingers around it. That's an innate behavior.

Which of these behaviors is innate? Which is learned?

Most animal offspring are born able to do more things than newborn human beings can do. Some animals, such as horses and goats, can walk just a few moments after they're born. Humans don't learn to walk until they're about a year old.

To look at another example, birds can build nests without lessons from their parents. Birds also form flocks innately. However, in bird species that can fly, a young bird must *learn* how to fly. It is born with the right kind of wings, but the young bird must practice flying. In the same way, a lion cub is born with the physical traits that will help it hunt. But it must learn how to hunt from its parents.

What factors determine the adaptations of living things?

Have you ever wondered why tigers have stripes, while lions are a solid tan color? It's because these two related species live in different environments. The lion lives on the African plains, where the tall grass is yellow-brown much of the year. The lion's tan coat blends in with that background. This trait makes it easier for the cat to sneak up on its prey.

The tiger lives in the sun-dappled forests of Asia. Black stripes on its orange coat help it blend in with the strips of light and shade in the forest. This trait, too, makes it easier for the cat to sneak up on its prey.

A trait that helps an organism survive in its environment is called an adaptation. The lion's coloring and the tiger's coloring are examples of physical adaptations.

Orange and black may be easy to see in a zoo, but they're hard to see in the tiger's natural environment.

Lions and tigers are closely related species that developed *different* adaptations in response to *different* habitats—places where they live and can find everything they need to survive. Sometimes living things that are not closely related may develop *similar* adaptations in response to *similar* habitats and ways of life.

For example, cacti in North America are spiny plants that store water, which helps them survive in deserts. In Africa, there are also spiny plants that store water and live in the desert. These plants are euphorbia, not cacti. They live half a world away from the North American cacti and are not closely related to them. But their environment is similar to the environment of the North American cacti.

Birds, flying insects, and bats all have wings. The three are not closely related, but aspects of their lives are similar.

How are form and function related?

An organism has the right body parts for the things those parts must do. Another way to say this is that form is suited to function. A great example is the elephant's trunk. It's an amazing adaptation of a nose. Its form is long and flexible, like an arm. The tip can grasp small objects, such as blades of grass. The form of the trunk is suited to its function—moving and grasping objects.

Form is suited to function in plants, too. For example, in some plants, the size, shape, and thickness of leaves help hold water. Tank bromeliads are especially good at holding water this way. These rainforest plants have big, thick leaves that form a bowl. The bowl can hold as much as 20 liters (5 gallons) of water.

The elephant's trunk can move over the ground in search of food and can also lift heavy objects.

The form of the owl butterfly's wings makes predators think twice about eating it.

Many adaptations help organisms catch prey. For example, the Venus flytrap is a plant that catches prey. The leaves have hairs that sense prey. A leaf snaps shut when a fly enters. Then the leaf gives off juices that digest the prey.

Foot adaptations help animals move from place to place. Some prairie animals, such as wild horses, have hooves that enable them to cross wide open spaces quickly. Aquatic animals such as ducks and otters have webbed feet for moving through water easily.

Other adaptations help organisms avoid predators. One type of butterfly has spots on its wings that look like the eyes of an owl. Small predators keep away, because they don't want to be attacked by an owl!

What are behavioral adaptations?

Physical adaptations aren't the only kind of adaptation. Organisms also have behavioral adaptations. A behavioral adaptation is a way of acting that helps an organism survive.

One behavioral adaptation is hunting in packs. Wolves and dogs have developed this adaptation. By hunting in packs, these animals can catch larger prey than by hunting alone. An example is the Arctic wolf. The prey of Arctic wolves includes animals that are larger than the wolves, such as musk oxen and caribou. The musk oxen have a behavioral adaptation of their own. When attacked, they form a circle, facing outward. Their huge horns face the attacker.

The defensive behavior of musk oxen wards off large predators such as wolves.

Canada geese follow their mother by instinct.

Much of the adaptive behavior of animals consists of instinct. An instinct is a behavior that is inherited and so does not have to be taught. For example, some types of newborn birds, such as graylag geese, follow the first creature that they see after they hatch. They act as if that creature were their mother. And in fact, its mother usually *is* the first thing that a hatchling sees when it comes out of its shell. Following the first animal that it sees keeps a hatchling from getting separated from its mother. Following its mother around also helps the young goose learn how to act like a proper goose. In this way, instincts and learned behaviors can support each other.

How do animals grow and develop?

As a baby, you were very different from what you are now, and you're very different now from what you will be as an adult. Life follows a series of stages called a life cycle. A life cycle goes from birth to youth to maturity to old age. The organism is physically different at each stage. Its behavior is different, too.

An animal's life cycle is a response to its environment. The cycle helps the species survive. For example, some turtle species bury their eggs in sand. This action hides the eggs from predators and helps more baby turtles hatch.

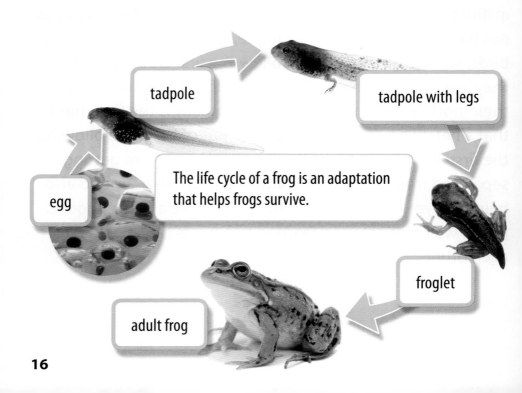

tadpole

tadpole with legs

The life cycle of a frog is an adaptation that helps frogs survive.

egg

froglet

adult frog

Some birds, such as swans, stay together for life. They raise many young together.

The life cycle of many species is adapted to protect the young. Emperor penguins, who live in the below-zero Antarctic, have a unique way of keeping their eggs warm. The male stands and balances the egg on his feet. He covers the egg with his warm pouch of skin and feathers. He stands for two months, in the fierce cold and wind, without eating anything. Just after the chick hatches, the female brings food for the chick.

Another life cycle adaptation is the way animals attract mates. Male birds of paradise perform complicated dances to attract females. Male peacocks show off their beautiful fanlike tails. Male and female swans do a display as a couple before beginning a lifetime together.

What is complete metamorphosis?

Some animals completely change their form from one stage of life to the next. This process is called metamorphosis. It occurs mostly in insects, though it also occurs in frogs and some other animals.

Complete metamorphosis in insects has four stages.

1. The egg is the beginning of life.
2. The larva is the young organism. It often crawls on the ground or on trees. Its main task in life is to eat and grow.
3. The pupa is the "resting stage." This stage is when the big change happens. The organism becomes motionless. It may build a covering to protect itself.
4. The adult is the full-grown stage. The adult breaks through the covering it made as a pupa. It can now reproduce.

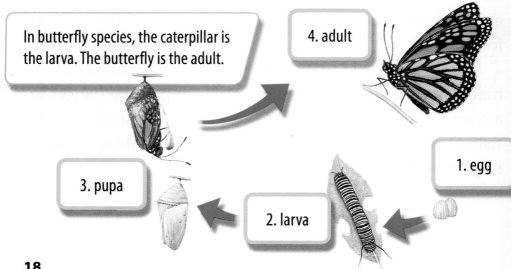

In butterfly species, the caterpillar is the larva. The butterfly is the adult.

4. adult

1. egg

2. larva

3. pupa

Beetles, flies, moths, butterflies, and bees go through complete metamorphosis.

beetle

moth

honeybee

The ground beetle in the United States undergoes complete metamorphosis. Most species of ground beetle lay their eggs in soil. The eggs hatch into larva that spend 1–2 years eating and growing. Ground beetle pupae undergo metamorphosis, or change, inside small chambers made out of soil. Often they undergo metamorphosis during the winter and emerge in the spring. They emerge as adults. The females lay eggs to begin the cycle again.

During metamorphosis, an organism eats different foods at different stages. The result is that the young and the adults don't compete for the same foods.

What is incomplete metamorphosis?

If there's such a thing as complete metamorphosis, is there also such a thing as incomplete metamorphosis? Yes, there is! The difference between the two is that the incomplete kind has only three stages, not four:

1. egg
2. nymph
3. adult

A nymph may look like a small version of the adult. It can't fly or reproduce, though. In some species, a hard shell protects the nymph. When the nymph grows big enough, it molts, or sheds its shell. Then it's an adult.

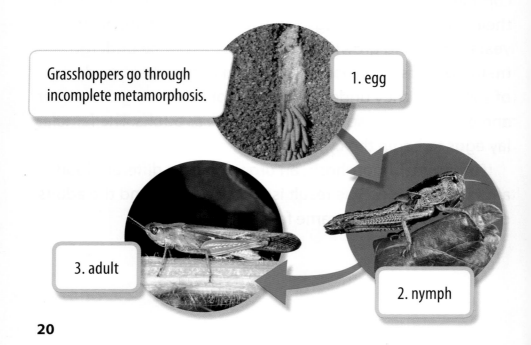

Grasshoppers go through incomplete metamorphosis.

1. egg

2. nymph

3. adult

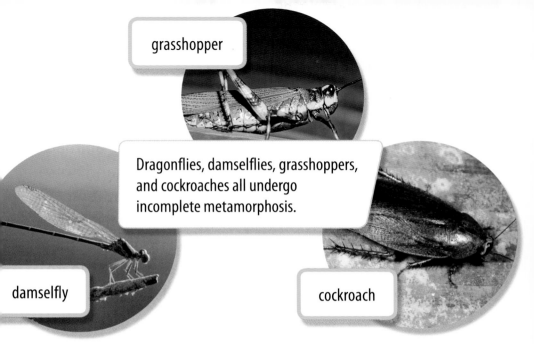

grasshopper

Dragonflies, damselflies, grasshoppers, and cockroaches all undergo incomplete metamorphosis.

damselfly

cockroach

One example of incomplete metamorphosis occurs in the dragonfly. Dragonfly females lay eggs in or near the water. The nymphs live in the water, where they hunt for food. As they grow, they molt several times. Each time, their wings are larger. Before their last molt, they crawl out of the water, often at night. Then they molt, and their hard casing drops to the ground, revealing adults with full-sized wings.

Like inherited and learned traits, and physical and behavioral traits, life cycles are a way of helping organisms survive.

Observe Animal Traits

Observe and record traits of two or more animals you're familiar with. Describe each trait, and note whether it is physical or behavioral; whether it is innate or learned; and how it helps the animal survive. Find the information in a book or on the Internet. Compare notes with classmates to learn about more animals and more animal traits.

Narrate a Metamorphosis

Imagine that you are an organism that undergoes metamorphosis. Pick any of the organisms mentioned in this book. Narrate what happens to you physically as you go through all the stages of your life cycle. Show how you behave at each stage.

Glossary

adaptation [ad·uhp·TAY·shuhn] A trait or characteristic that helps an organism survive.

complete metamorphosis [kum·PLEET met·uh·MAWR·fuh·sis] A complex change that most insects undergo that includes larva and pupa stages.

dominant trait [DAHM·ih·nuhnt TRAYT] A trait that appears if an organism has one factor for that trait.

gene [JEEN] The part of cells that controls or influences inherited traits such as hair color and eye color.

incomplete metamorphosis [in·kum·PLEET met·uh·MAWR·fuh·sis] Developmental change in some insects in which a nymph hatches from an egg and gradually develops into an adult.

inherited traits [in·HAIR·it·ed TRAYTS] Characteristics passed from parents to their offspring.

innate behaviors [in•AYT bee•HAYV•yuhrz] Behaviors that an organism is born with.

instinct [IN•stinkt] A behavior that an organism inherits and knows how to do without being taught.

learned behaviors [LERND bee•HAYV•yuhrz] Behaviors that an animal doesn't begin life with but develops as a result of experience or by observing other animals.

life cycle [LYF SY•kuhl] The stages that a living thing passes through as it grows and changes.

recessive trait [ree•SES•iv TRAYT] A trait that appears only if an organism has two factors for that trait.